# CALIFORNIA

## THE LAND ▲ THE PEOPLE ▲ THE CITIES

OREGON

IDAHO

Redwood
National
Park

▲ Mt. Shasta

Eureka

C O A S T A L

Sacramento River

Lassen Peak

S I E R R A

NEVADA

Lake
Tahoe

Sacramento Valley

Russian River

Sacramento

Mono
Lake

P A C I F I C

Point
Reyes
National
Seashore

Yosemite
National
Park

Berkeley

San Francisco Bay

Oakland

San Francisco

San Jose

San Joaquin Valley

N E V A D A

Monterey

R A N G E

Kings
Canyon
National
Park

Carmel

Salinas River

Fresno

Death
Valley

▲ Mt. Whitney

Sequoia
National
Park

O C E A N

S

San Luis Obispo

Lake
Havasu

Santa Barbara

S

Joshua Tree
National Monument

Los Angeles

ARIZONA

Salton
Sea

San Diego

MEXICO

# CALIFORNIA

## THE LAND · THE PEOPLE · THE CITIES

PAMELA THOMAS

PHOTOGRAPHY BY
VIESTI ASSOCIATES

MALLARD PRESS

MALLARD PRESS
AN IMPRINT OF BDD PROMOTIONAL BOOK COMPANY, INC.
666 FIFTH AVENUE · NEW YORK · NEW YORK 10103

**A FRIEDMAN GROUP BOOK**

Published by MALLARD PRESS
An imprint of BDD Promotional Book Company, Inc.
666 Fifth Avenue
New York, New York 10103

Mallard Press and its accompanying design and logo are trademarks of BDD
Promotional Book Company, Inc.

ISBN 0-7924-5303-4

CALIFORNIA
The Land, The People, The Cities
was prepared and produced by
Michael Friedman Publishing Group, Inc.
15 West 26th Street
New York, New York 10010

Editor: Sharyn Rosart
Designer: Stephanie Bart-Horvath
Photography Editor: Christopher Bain

Typeset by The Interface Group, Inc.
Color separations by Scantrans Pte. Ltd.
Printed and bound in Hong Kong by Leefung-Asco Printers Ltd.

To my California brother, Steve Thomas, and
his California kids, Stephanie and Brad

# CONTENTS

8

# INTRODUCTION

CALIFORNIA IS AMERICA'S "great legs," the long, gloriously golden extremities of the great goddess of the New World. Founded in the early days of European exploration of the North American continent (British explorer Francis Drake landed his *The Golden Hinde* at Drake's Bay, north of what is now San Francisco, in 1594), California was controlled for over two hundred years by the Spanish. It came under American control almost simultaneously with the discovery of gold in 1848 and then enjoyed a boom in the 1850s. California grew quickly and steadily but did not come into maturity until the mid-twentieth century.

By 1964, when California emerged as the most populous state in the United States, it was considered by many to be not only the most popular, but perhaps the most distinctive, state in the country, with a personality all its own. When outsiders—be they Europeans, Asians, or New Yorkers—conjure up visions of California in their mind's eye, they think of hot tubs, roller skaters, suntanned bathing beauties, glamorous movie stars, miles of beaches, and billions of automobiles racing along California's myriad freeways. For several decades, especially during the years of California's most incredible growth, between 1920 and 1980, when the population exploded tenfold, California was synonymous with "the good life." With sunny skies, warm days, cheap real estate, excellent schools, and a healthy economy—California was—as writer/environmentalist Wallace Stegner once described it "America, only more so."

Today, California suffers from the excesses of its fame. Environmental problems such as smog, eroding beaches, mud slides, forest fires, and earthquakes are making those who might move to California think twice, and are even forcing native Californians to consider leaving. Overpopulation in the large cities has resulted in major problems with drugs, crime, and disease. And traffic jams are legendary.

Nevertheless, California is still considered to be the most alluring and fascinating of America's fifty states—and for good reason. Its uniqueness lies not only in breathtaking variety, but in the extremes of its beauty. In fact, much of California can be discussed in the superlative.

California claims as its own one of the most beautiful mountain ranges in the country, the Sierra Nevadas, in the midst of which rises continental America's highest peak, Mount Whitney. California cares for America's most mythical desert, Death Valley, which surrounds the country's lowest geologic point. California has the longest stretch of Pacific shoreline in the United States, and perhaps the most splendid beaches.

Its cities are also unique and marvelous. No one can visit San Francisco without falling in love with it. No one can drive through Los Angeles without being impressed—by its vitality, its complexity, and in some parts, its beauty. No one can vacation in San Diego without agreeing with that town's unabashed proclamation of itself as "America's Favorite City."

California natives—and today, at last, many Californians are true natives, not pioneers—are equally varied, remarkable, and unique. Whether one is talking about a Santa Monica surfer or a Mendocino logger, a Hollywood starlet or a world-renowned Napa Valley chef, one is discussing a very special sort of American, not only a product of his or her environment, but an active participant in making California one of America's treasures.

California is known as the Golden State, and its flower is the golden poppy. This golden appellation came about as a result of the notorious gold fields that attracted thousands of miners and sparked a rush for land in the mid-nineteenth century. But the nickname also suggests the brilliant sunshine, the warm, glowing inhabitants, and the golden grass on California pastures in the autumn. Most of all, it suggests the valuable prize that provides such a spectacular finish to the American continent.

# THE LAND

Describing the physical features of the California landscape is an awesome task. California is the third largest state in the United States (after Alaska and Texas), covering an area of 158,706 square miles (911,033 square km). Not only is California vast, but unlike either Alaska or Texas, the entire region is a study in variety and extremes.

The high Sierra Nevada mountains rise near the eastern border, with Mount Whitney, the highest peak in the continental United States, looming 14,495 feet (4,418 m) above sea level. In stark contrast to the mountains, much of Southern California is desert and boasts the legendary Death Valley, with the nation's lowest geographic point (282 feet [85 m] below sea level) and highest recorded temperature (134 degrees Fahrenheit [56° C] in July 1913). Rocky, magnificently forested cliffs and sandy beaches line the shore of the Pacific Ocean, the state's western border, and the nation's most fertile

**THE VIEW FROM BIG SUR,**
*looking south (previous page).*

**A LONE BRISTLECONE**
*(or brisling) pine rises from*
*the desert like a piece of*
*freestanding driftwood. These*
*trees grow in a 28,000-acre*
*(11,300-ha) area of Inyo*
*National Forest, near the*
*desert on the east side of*
*the Sierras.*

valley runs down California's center.

California boasts a cornucopia of America's most magnificent natural wonders, including the eerie Mono Lake, Death Valley, the General Sherman sequoia tree (the world's largest living thing), the bizarre Joshua Tree National Monument, Big Sur, and the Redwood National Forest.

The California landscape can be divided into approximately eight sectors, or regions: the Northern Coast, the Far Northeast, Wine Country, the Sierra Nevadas, the Central Coast, the Central Valley, Southern California, and Baja California. Each region is unique, so different from the others, in fact, that each could be a separate "state" unto itself. If anything, the regions are a vast study in contrasts, with each differing in climate, history, topography, and temperament. These contrasts are what make California special.

## The Northern Coast—Redwood Country

Stretching almost four hundred miles (640 km), from the southern border of Oregon to the San Francisco Bay area, the so-called Northern Coast rises up from the sea and is still largely unspoiled and magnificently beautiful.

The Northern Coast is home to one of California's renowned treasures, Redwood National Park. The weather is variable and moody in redwood country. Autumn is without a doubt its finest season, when the air turns brisk, the sky glows bright blue, and the flora colors brighten. But spring and summer are also beautiful, and the windflowers, which bloom from March until August, are spectacular. The Northern Coast is almost as well-known for its excellent fishing, hiking,

A GIANT SEQUOIA,
*swathed in sunshine and snow,*
*stands as the epitome of*
*beauty amid the natural life of*
*the Sierra Nevada.*

A PANORAMIC VIEW OF *the forested mountains of Inyo National Forest near Lee Vining, California.*

and backpacking as it is for its spectacular scenery.

Although redwood country actually extends south from Oregon as far as Monterey, Redwood National Park itself begins just south of the Oregon border and reaches down the coast for about forty miles (64 km). Many of the best specimens of *Sequoia sempervirens*, the tall, graceful species of redwood (the California state tree), are found in the park. The oldest known redwood was some 2,200 years old when cut down in the 1930s. The tallest—indeed, the tallest tree of any kind in the world, at 368 feet (110 m)—is also located there. The fabulous Avenue of Giants, a thirty-three-mile (53-km) scenic route, Lady Bird Johnson Grove, and Tall Trees Grove are especially attractive redwood regions.

Logging and fishing built Eureka, California, the largest city in the Northern Coast's Humboldt County, and they still constitute its main industries. Eureka is perhaps the most important town along the Northern Coast, and it marks the midway point between San Francisco and Portland, Oregon. Its charming hotels and inns and fine restaurants make it an ideal stopping-off point for travelers. Ubiquitous Victorian architecture, with brightly colored turrets, spires, and gables, can be seen throughout the town. Many structures are well preserved, especially the Carson Mansion, which was built in 1886 and is one of the most famous edifices in the state.

The Mendocino County coastline runs south of Redwood National Park, roughly from Rockport to the Gualala River. Many think this area resembles New England, because it has a certain nineteenth-century charm and natural beauty. But the area is rougher than gentle New England—more Western—with a turbulent surf, moody clouds, frequent fog, a rugged coastline, and dark, cool trees covering the hills. Narrow, crooked roads preserve the relative remoteness of the quaint town of Mendocino.

Mendocino's buildings with weathered wooden shingles and sloping roofs recall a New England village. The town was founded in 1852 by transplanted Easterners who thought the exposed location a natural site for milling. These original settlers have long since been superceded by writers, artists, and artisans.

Logging is still an important industry along the

*THE CARSON MANSION in Eureka, California, a hodge-podge of turrets, gables, and moldings, was built in 1886 for lumber baron, William Carson. The house now serves as a men's club, but remains a fine example of California Victorian architecture.*

16

**THE ABUNDANT WILDLIFE IN CALIFORNIA IS AS FASCINATING AS**
*its waterfalls, domes, lush meadows, and dramatic beaches.*

Mendocino coast. The loggers and artists have combined to create a fascinating mix. In 1974, Mendocino County "seceded" from the state and formed its own "state," which was called "Northern California." However, it was noted that the secession was unlikely to worry anyone much: Loss of the county would not be noticed until the fog lifted—and there was no chance of that happening soon!

The neighboring Sonoma County coastline runs south from the mouth of the Gualala River to Bodega Bay, just above Point Reyes. The Sonoma coastline is fringed with a series of remarkable beach parks and awesome scenery, and it boasts Fort Ross, the last surviving remnant of the nineteenth-century Russian settlements in California. Fort Ross was the North American outpost for Russian fur traders in the 1800s.

The Marin County shore, just north of San Francisco, marks the southern tip of California's Northern Coast. Despite its close proximity to a sophisticated urban area, it retains a feeling of remoteness and wild splendor.

Point Reyes Peninsula is an ideal place. Wildflowers bloom from February to July. The peninsula is actually an island separated from the mainland by the San Andreas Fault. As a result of earthquakes, the land on the west side of Point Reyes has moved about twenty feet (6 m). The bay that runs along the south of Point Reyes is known as Drake's Bay, since Sir Francis Drake landed his ship, *The Golden Hinde,* there in 1579.

## The Far Northeast—Mount Shasta and the Cascades

The Far Northeast sector of California is sometimes referred to as a "northern wonderland," with its majestic mountains, pristine lakes, verdant valleys, and rushing streams. The Cascade mountain range descends

19

THE SHASTA REGION, IN *California's Northern Coast regions, is a hiker's and climber's paradise, with snow-capped peaks, sulfur pools, craters, and lava beds. It is a land of contrasts.*

**MIGHTY MOUNT**
*Shasta, which rises 14,151 feet (4,313 m) above Strawberry Valley, is the most significant natural sight for over one hundred miles (160 km) and is considered sacred by many who live near its foothills.*

into California at this point. These rugged peaks, combined with two other mountain ranges, the Klamath-Scott and the Warner, make this region one of the most remote areas of the state. Some parts of it are accessible only to hikers and backpackers.

Mighty Mount Shasta is the central and highest peak in the region. With its slightly smaller sister, Shastina, Mount Shasta serves as a magnificent focal point, with awesome snow-capped peaks and icy slopes.

Mount Lassen, another important peak, well known because it erupted in 1915, looms over a valley of sulfur pools, craters, chimneys, and cones that make up Lassen Volcanic National Park. Other areas dotted with volcanic plains and caves, including Lava Beds National Monument, can be found in this quadrant of the state. Tule Lake and Lower Klamath Wildlife Refuge, north of Lava Beds, serve as a way station for the largest concentration of waterfowl on the North American continent. Castle Crags State Park and McArthur Memorial Park also offer natural sights, each more breathtaking than the last. Burney Falls, in McArthur Park, is to some the most beautiful natural phenomenon in California.

Like the Northern Coast, the Far Northeast region is an outdoor-lover's paradise. Fishing is excellent in the lakes surrounding the main town, Redding. The mountain lakes and streams are rich with salmon, trout, steelhead chinook, and other catches virtually year-round. Boating is almost as popular as fishing, and hiking is the most prevalent sport of all.

*MOUNT SHASTA IS volcanic in origin and is composed of two cones— Shasta, the large peak, and Shastina, a smaller cone that rises to the west of the larger Shasta. Five glaciers lie to the eastern and northeastern edges of the mountain, rising to a height of about 10,000 feet (3000 m).*

Some forty miles (64 km) northeast of San Francisco lies an area that has become synonymous with California wine. Napa Valley, which lies between two ridges, has spawned the United States' most famous wineries, including large firms such as Mondavi, Christian Brothers, and Charles Krug, in addition to smaller, and often exquisite, wineries such as Sutter Home and Château Montelena. But the wineries of Sonoma Valley, a few miles east on the other side of the Mayacama Mountains, are equally marvelous. Since the early 1970s, the wineries of the Russian River valleys—such as Alexander Valley and Dry Creek Valley—have also become important.

But it is Napa Valley, the luxurious valley that runs for about twenty miles (32 km) from the town of Napa north to the village of Calistoga, that wine connoisseurs have come to cherish most. The narrow roads through the valley (State Route 128 and the parallel road, the Silverado Trail) string together a veritable necklace of now-famous towns—especially Yountville, Rutherford, Saint Helena, Silverado, and Calistoga—and wineries.

Even the little, unassuming Oakville Grocery, standing like an old-fashioned general store in the midst of a deceptively modest country town, has achieved a certain celebrity among chefs, gourmands, and food critics across the country. The Napa Valley Olive Oil Manufactory, along with its gourmet food shop, is another center that has enjoyed "fame from association."

From the nineteenth-century elegance of the Beringer Winery to the lavish modern complex built by Domaine Chandon, the wineries reflect the personalities of their product, whether rich, sophisticated, or mellow. In fact, California winemaking has become so sophisticated that wine is produced throughout the state. Sonoma Valley has produced such fine vineyards as Kenwood, Sebastiani, and Glen Ellen. Sonoma, the city, has Simi and Korbel. Even as far north as Mendocino County, such nice wines as Parducci and Fetzer are produced. But Napa Valley was the birthplace of the great California wines, and Napa remains supreme.

LUSH NAPA VALLEY
*grapes, particularly the*
*Cabernet Sauvignon, the*
*Chardonnay, and the Pinot*
*Noir, produce some of the*
*finest wines in the world.*

**MOST OF CALIFORNIA'S** *renowned vineyards are clustered in the Napa Valley and in the somewhat less touristy Sonoma Valley. Here is a glimpse of the Sebastiani Family Vineyard at Sonoma.*

**RUBY BASIN IS ONE OF THE** *many magnificent basins formed amid the peaks of the High Sierras.*

The Sierra Nevada mountain range, California's backbone, is one of the steepest and most physically stunning mountain ranges in the continental United States. In the early years of California's development, the Sierras seemed to form a wall against the onslaught of newcomers. Nevertheless, pioneers and wanderers were able to break through (or else found the passage through Owens Valley), and the new settlers quickly saw the wealth to be made from logging the giant sequoias that grew abundantly on the mountains.

In the late nineteenth century, naturalist John Muir, appalled by the logging that threatened the giant sequoias, wrote extensively of the beauty of these California wonders and lobbied to protect them from further destruction. (Muir also founded the Sierra Club, which remains profoundly influential to environmental protection measures to this day.) Muir convinced the United States Congress to establish Yosemite National Park and Sierra National Park to protect the trees—and all the other wildlife of the area. Later, other enthusiastic environmentalists created additional reserves, including Inyo National Forest, Kings Canyon National Park, Sequoia National Park, Sequoia National Forest, and Death Valley National Park.

Stretching some 450 miles (720 km) from Lake Almanor to the Mojave Desert, the high Sierra terrain is varied, with the western slope rising gradually from brush and chaparral pines into high, snow-capped peaks. Meadows, glaciers, rivers, and lakes punctuate the landscape, and the entire region is habitat to hundreds of animal species, including bears, deer, mountain lions, and bobcats, not to mention a wide variety of birds and fish. The eastern slope, especially the Sierra Crest, which runs along the eastern border of Sequoia National Park, is rugged and forbidding, but one of the world's most beautiful sights.

Yosemite National Park is the most famous of the Sierra region's natural parks—and for good reason. With its towering domes and cliffs, graceful yet powerful waterfalls, and verdant meadows, it is truly one of the great wonders of the world. Most travelers tour the Yosemite Valley, cut through by the seven-mile (11-km)

29

*EL CAPITAN, AT 7,589 feet (2,313 m), is the largest granite monolith in the world, rising powerfully from verdant meadows. Other spectacular sights nearby include Cathedral Rocks, Three Brothers, Sentinel Rock, and Half Dome.*

**THE DISTINCTIVE BEAUTY**
*of Yosemite National Park, the
Sierra's most famous treasure,
has much to do with its
towering yet graceful cliffs and
its glorious cascading
waterfalls.*

THE YOSEMITE VALLEY, CREATED
*by the Merced River, is a vision of*
*tranquility with its stately trees, lush*
*meadows, groves of pines and oaks, and*
*wide variety of flowers, ferns, and grasses.*

ALTHOUGH THE
*Yosemite Valley is neither the deepest nor the longest valley in the Sierra range, its glacial gorges have the sheerest walls and the most distinctive forms (left). Here an experienced climber scales a stunning valley wall.*

A ROCK CLIMBER
*scales one of the mountain peaks on the spectacular east side of the Sierra Nevadas, near Bishop, California, in the heart of Owens Valley (opposite page).*

Merced River, but that section forms only a small part of Yosemite's magnificent natural wonders.

One such phenomenon is Mono Lake, which was formed by fresh water from streams and springs that drained into a bed and then evaporated, leaving behind a mineral-rich lake. No fish can survive there, but other forms of life, such as shrimp, brine flies, and algae, flourish. Where the springs meet the salty water, remarkable white tufa towers have formed from the springs' mineral deposits.

Kings Canyon National Park, Sequoia National Park, Inyo National Park, and Sequoia National Forest, although not quite as famous as Yosemite, all claim their fair share of natural wonders, not to mention exquisite beauty. Glacier-carved Kings Canyon boasts an astonishing array of cliffs and waterfalls, breathtaking vistas, and the deepest canyon walls in the country. From Sequoia National Park, the Sierra Crest lifts itself to its greatest heights, with several 14,000-foot (4,270-m) peaks along the park's eastern border, including Mount Whitney. Sequoia National Forest, situated south of the Kings Canyon and Sequoia national parks, covers the southern tip of the Sierra Nevadas.

Growing with lush exuberance in all of these large parks are the most massive trees on earth—the giant sequoias. One of the most famous is the General Sherman tree, the world's largest (though not tallest) tree, which is 102 feet (30 m) in circumference, 36$^1$/$_2$ feet (11 m) thick, and 275 feet (84 m) high. Despite their individual grandeur, it is the trees seen en masse that create the spell of the Sierras.

Many people believe that the impact of the Sierra Nevadas is best appreciated as it turns toward that infamous desert running south and east of the range, the vast Mojave. For many, this desert holds a special mystique, with its rugged hills and rocky terrain, colorful sunsets and surprisingly lush wildflowers.

Death Valley is part of the magic of the Mojave, and it has made its mark as a result of its great size, its extremes in terrain and climate, and its colorful history. For fourteen square miles (36 square km), the valley forms the lowest point in the Western Hemisphere, at 238 feet (72 m) below sea level. The salt beds in this area are equally remarkable, while nearby Telescope Peak

37

**SUNRISE OVER MONO**
*Lake, at the north end of the Sierra Nevada mountain range is a beautiful sight. Mark Twain once referred to this "inland sea" as the "Dead Sea of the West."*

**INYO NATIONAL FOREST**
*lies southeast of Yosemite. "Inyo" means "dwelling place of the great spirits" in Indian language, and the beautiful forests and cool lakes of the park make the name easy to comprehend.*

**THE SHIFTING SANDS OF DEATH VALLEY ARE**
*just one of California's spectacular natural wonders.*

rises to 11,049 feet (3,368 m) above sea level and is one of the highest points on the desert.

This entire region of the Sierras, including the spectacular desert that is formed at the southern edge of the mountain range, is not only one of California's great scenic prizes and an American treasure, but one of the greatest natural wonders in the world.

## The Central Coast and Big Sur

One is left breathless by the Sierra Nevadas, yet amazingly, the Central Coast of California is equally spectacular. Although Route 1 is a man-made accomplishment of sorts—and a supremely California wonder at that—the scenery one can observe driving up the California coast makes one appreciate the ever-present automobile and in some cases, the roads on which it can be driven.

The great jewel of the Central Coast is Big Sur. At first glance it seems a mere hill, but somehow the precipice created by that hill, the crashing waves below it, the glorious beach that runs along it, and the mysterious weather surrounding it, make it one of the most magnificent "hills" known to man.

Until the 1960s, Big Sur was one of the more remote areas of the California coastline. It is majestically beautiful, but the elements are fierce there. The weather is changeable, with dark, looming clouds rolling in, the threat of treacherous thunderstorms, and incredibly high winds whipping along the high hills and rocky beaches. Yet this sometimes-perilous climate only adds to Big Sur's majesty and mystery. The rocky beaches are assaulted by crashing waves, and the hills look as if they were ordered by Hollywood for a scene from *Wuthering Heights,* American style. The flora are abundant, and the scrub land beautiful in its natural harshness. No village has cropped up within a stone's throw of Big Sur, because Big Sur is about nature, not about civilization.

In many ways, the Central Coast can best be described by its more inhabited areas. Some twenty miles (32 km) north of remote Big Sur lies the glamorous Monterey Peninsula.

THE GIANT FOREST,
*the focal point of Sequoia National Park, glories in the largest concentration of giant sequoia trees in the world. Their unbelievable size becomes apparent when they are compared with an everyday pine tree—or to a human being.*

THIS IS JUST ONE OF
*several falls, including Roaring River Falls and Mist Falls, that make the Cedar Grove area inside King's Canyon one of the most spectacular sections of Sequoia National Park.*

41

**RIDERS ON HORSEBACK**
*enjoy the sunrise and the
majestic beauty along the
magnificent beach at Big Sur.*

*THE NORTHERN COAST OF California, with its crashing waves, jagged rocks, and elegant cypress trees, retains much of its ancient natural beauty.*

*MAJESTIC BIG SUR IS ONE of California's most distinctive natural wonders, with its darkly looming hills, glorious beaches, and rich treasure of flora and fauna (far right).*

The town of Monterey was settled in 1770, the first of Spain's four California presidios and the second of the Franciscan Friars' twenty-one Alta California missions. In fact, until the mid-nineteenth century, Monterey was California's liveliest and most important settlement. It was the Spanish capital of Alta California, the Mexican capital of the region in 1822, and the American capital in 1846. After the discovery of gold, in 1848, the capital was moved to San Francisco, and finally, Sacramento.

Today, Monterey is a modern town of about thirty thousand people and is noted as a fish processing center, a business that was originally made notorious in John Steinbeck's novel *Cannery Row*. The booming—and problematic—industry died when the nearby waters became "fished out," but Monterey has turned the old Cannery Row and Fisherman's Wharf into important tourist attractions. In addition, Monterey houses America's largest exhibit aquarium. It has also been home to the star-studded and world-renowned Monterey Jazz Festival since 1958.

Pacific Grove, a sort of suburb of Monterey, lies a few miles out on the northwest corner of the peninsula. Just south of Pacific Grove begins the "Seventeen-Mile Drive," one of the most scenic routes in California, which runs through the Del Monte Forest and along the coast of the peninsula shoreline. Pebble Beach, the famed golf course, lies along the peninsula's south shore. (In fact, the Monterey Peninsula is known as the "golf capital of the world," claiming more than a dozen fine courses.)

Carmel-by-the Sea, or just plain Carmel, completes the Monterey Peninsula. Carmel has always prided itself as a simple village by the ocean, even when it was first settled by Father Junipero Serra. Even today, the houses have no street numbers, and mail is still picked up at the post office. Trees are permitted to grow through sidewalks or in the middle of the street. The beach is calm and beautiful. Yet Carmel is, in fact, one of the most affluent and sophisticated "villages" in all of California.

Beyond the Monterey Peninsula, the Central Coast, with its breathtaking beaches, looming hills, and temperamental climate, weaves somewhat peacefully south. It is interrupted only twice in any major way by human or urban intrusion, but both are fascinating in their own ways.

San Simeon, the 123-acre (50-ha) estate built in 1922 by newspaper magnate William Randolph Hearst, sits regally on the coast overlooking the Pacific. He called the estate La Cuesta Encantada, or "The Enchanted Hill." Given the surrounding scenery, it was a name well chosen. La Casa Grande, the estate's main house, is a study in Hollywood opulence, but somehow its magnificence fits.

Santa Barbara is the only city of note on the southern portion of the Central Coast. Santa Barbara's first inhabitants, the Chumash people, lived off the resources of the region's calm waters. The Spanish missionaries chose Santa Barbara as a site for a mission in 1782. In the 1920s, the city boomed when a large oil deposit was discovered, but was leveled soon after by a powerful earthquake in 1925. The residents—including many wealthy southern Californians eager to escape the urban blight of Los Angeles—rebuilt the town as a tribute to Spanish colonial style, forbidding the building of a freeway and allowing no buildings to be more than two storeys high. As a result, Santa Barbara, abutting ever-sprawling Los Angeles, is where California's central coast comes to a halt.

**SKELETAL VESTIGES OF** *Gold Rush days, like this abandoned house, can still be found in the valleys near Sacramento.*

## The Central Valley

The Central Valley lies between the Sierra Nevada Mountains on the east, the Coast Range on the west, the Tehachapi Mountains to the south, and the foothills of the Cascades and the northern Coast Range to the north. It extends 465 miles (748 km) from north to south and ranges from thirty to sixty miles (50 to 100 km) wide. The Central Valley is California's "fruit basket," a lush valley that permits California to rank first among all American states in agriculture. Specifically, it is the leading center for the production of fruits, nuts, vegetables, cotton, wheat, rice, and livestock.

The valley is actually two valleys—the Sacramento (through which runs the Sacramento River) and the San Joaquin (named for the river that runs through it). Once called the Badlands because of its rugged, arid terrain, the Central Valley was changed by irrigation early in the twentieth century and is now the most fertile farmland in the world.

The Sacramento Valley "grew up" during the Gold Rush days, when river steamers and sailing schooners on the Sacramento and Feather rivers connected such communities as Marysville and Red Bluff to Sacramento. After the gold was panned out, the miners got practical and began growing grain along the river, a crop that remains the valley's chief product. Later, farmers established citrus groves and other fruit orchards, and began to grow alfalfa, vegetables, cotton, and sugar beets—all lucrative crops.

The city of Sacramento, which had already boomed as a result of the Gold Rush, emerged as an important agricultural center, but other quiet towns along the banks of the Sacramento River have changed little since the early 1900s.

The San Joaquin Valley, south of the Sacramento Valley, was developed a bit later. A twist of nature and climate allows grapes of maximum sugar to grow abundantly here. As a result, the towns of Lodi and Fresno have become famous for their production of sweet wines. Stockton is the main "port" city in the valley. Like Sacramento, it came into being in the 1850s, but later found its true worth as an agricultural center and a link to San Francisco Bay.

Although it has a feisty and romantic history due to its links to the Gold Rush days, the Central Valley lacks the scenic drama of California's other regions—the rugged, snow-capped peaks of the north, the crashing waves and melancholy fog of the coast, or the lush flora and fauna and breathtaking crests of the Sierras. Yet California depends on the Central Valley's resources in many ways, and the state would be lost without it.

## Southern California

South of the Central Valley and the Sierras lies a region as different from the rest of California as Spain is from the Scottish Highlands. The Mojave Desert, which adds a flourish to the base of the Sierras, is actually more a part of the Southern California terrain than it is related to the majestic mountains. In fact, most of Southern California is a desert that includes a chain of national parks and natural monuments.

The most famous is the Anza-Borrego Desert State Park, which covers over six hundred thousand acres (240,000 ha) of barren flats and rocky slopes and is the largest state park in the continental United States. The park is named for Juan Bautista de Anza, who led the first European expedition into the area and settled at Borrego Springs, where a city encircled by the park now exists. Prior to Anza's arrival, Indians had successfully inhabited various parts of the desert. Nevertheless, most of the desert remains untamed and, with its brown and red hues, it is notable for its heat, vast silence, and the impression of an almost unholy peace.

Another important park is the Joshua Tree National Monument, which forms a link between the Mojave and Sonoran deserts. The Mormons, when they crossed the desert, were fascinated by the unique yucca trees that grew there. They saw the bent limbs as symbolic of the prophet Joshua welcoming wanderers to the promised land.

This area is also known for the odd and ubiquitous rock formations that dot the landscape. Many underground springs exist, creating oases and groves of palms, including those known as Twenty-nine Palms, Forty-nine Palms, Cottonwood Spring, and Lost Palms. Perhaps because of the hidden water, the springtime

49

THE REGION NEAR
*Indio is known as the "Date*
*Capital of the United States"*
*because of its 200,000-plus*
*date palm trees, which yield*
*about forty million pounds*
*(18 million kg) of dates of*
*many varieties. The Indio*
*National Date Fesitval is*
*a highlight event.*

**THE JOSHUA TREE**
*National Monument, which lies at the edge of two great deserts, is a land of beautiful desert studded with trees, plants, and in spring, wildflowers.*

flowering of cacti and desert wildflowers is particularly spectacular.

South of the Joshua Tree National Monument lies the twenty-five-mile- (40-km-) long Salton Sea, a below-sea-level saltwater lake that was once an inland sea. Now a great center for fishing and boating, it is a remarkable "oasis" surrounded by desert.

Indio, California, in the midst of the desert, is the "Date Capital of the United States"—not a singles mecca, but the site of one of the richest date groves in the world.

The hub of the Southern California desert, surrounded by mountains, is the town of Palm Springs, an oasis that from all appearances has nothing to do with nature and yet, in a sense, has everything to do with it. Palm Springs is known as the "Oasis of the Stars," Hollywood's watering hole, because such famous entertainers as Bing Crosby, Bob Hope, and Frank Sinatra established estates in the town. In recent years, Sonny Bono, former husband and partner to actress/singer/celebrity Cher, has been a very popular mayor of Palm Springs. Established in the 1930s as a Hollywood publicity stunt, the resort has been a glamor spot for over fifty years. However, in recent years, the bloom has come off the desert flower, as students flock to Palm Springs during school breaks, turning it for a time into what some natives refer to as "the Fort Lauderdale of the West."

By a fluke of fate, the largest land-owning entity in Palm Springs is the Agua Caliente band of Chauilla Native American Indians. The tribe gravitated there because of the abundant springs in the foothill canyon. The Indians were given leases to the land and now basically "rent" it to the hoteliers and rich homeowners.

But it is nature, ultimately, that created Palm Springs and keeps the city the paradise it remains. The San Jacinto Mountains and several other smaller mountains shelter the town, allowing residents and visitors to enjoy ideal warm weather and very little smog almost year-round. Condominiums clustered around luxurious swimming pools, elegant shops, and delicious restaurants make this one of the most popular resort spots in America.

53

DEATH VALLEY NATIONAL
Monument, which runs southeast of the Sierra Nevadas, is
unique in its extremes of heat
and elevation and notorious
for being "unsuitable" for any
living thing.

# THE PEOPLE

**C**alifornians are a distinctive group. Even to other Americans, they often seem a bit foreign—a world apart. "California girls," as the Beach Boys wail, are tall and willowy, with sun-kissed skin and long blond tresses. If they live in "the Valley," they speak in California "tongues," a sing-song dialect decipherable only by their peers. California men, too, are considered different. Laid back, easygoing, "with it," and always, but *always*, trim and handsome. A recently published etiquette book states clearly that one should never wear leisure sweats when traveling on airplanes. This book must have been written by a Californian, because such a thought would never occur to any American male except a Los Angeles mogul on his way to a meeting in New York.

These images form the myth of the twentieth-century Californian. The reality is much richer, more varied, and rooted in the

*BODIE, CALIFORNIA, now an authentic ghost town, boasted 10,000 inhabitants, 65 saloons, and one homicide per day in its heyday as a mining town around 1880.*

state's history, development and landscape.

When California established statehood on September 9, 1850, its entire population was less than 100,000 people. By 1990, that number had grown to almost thirty million, 20 times the state's population of a century before and almost twice its population in 1964, when it became the most populous state in the Union.

The people who have created this enormous growth are by no means all tall, blond gods and goddesses. In fact, the population of California is a true melting pot of races, cultures, and personalities.

## A Few Nuggets of History

Although Sir Francis Drake, an English explorer, landed in Northern California in the late 1500s, it was the Spanish conquistadors who perceived that they had found someplace special. They called the land "California," after a treasure island in a popular Spanish tale, a mythical land full of gold jewels and tall bronze-colored Amazons. Little did they know that their myth would one day become a reality.

Although the Spanish conquerors sailed up and down the beautiful coast for decades, California was not vigorously colonized until the coming of the Franciscan padres from Mexico in the 1770s. During the years that the scruffy Colonial soldiers were fighting the battles of Bunker Hill and Valley Forge on the East Coast, mission communities such as San Diego, Monterey, Carmel, San Francisco, and San Jose were being established by the Spanish up the California coast. Led by Father Junipero Serra, the padres arrived to convert and aid thousands of Native Americans. When Mexico achieved independence from Spain, in 1821, it turned California into a colony. The mission system was dissolved in 1833.

Almost immediately, the Mexican government repartitioned the Franciscan lands among private citizens, and this resulted briefly in the rise of the aristocratic cattle raiser, the *ranchero*. Roaming the open ranges, and presiding over vast ranches, these men soon dominated the West Coast and created a mythology that would be repeated, although with perhaps less dash, sixty years later in the Plains states, where it was called the "Wild West."

In 1841, the first U.S. settlers began migrating overland to set up their own farms in California's inland valleys. One such group, the Donner party, became infamous because they were trapped by an early snow near Donner Lake, in Northern California, and resorted to cannibalism—half the party perished—in order to survive. In 1846, after groups of U.S. settlers staged a revolt against the Mexican rancheros and proclaimed California's independence, U.S. soldiers arrived and occupied what the settlers referred to as the "Bear Flag Republic." (California's state flag remains a "bear flag.")

At the end of the Mexican-American War, in 1848, Mexico ceded California and the rest of its Western holdings to the United States, with the exception of Baja California, the southern peninsula of California, which to this day belongs to Mexico. The treaty's timing could not have been more fortuitous. Literally within days of the signing of the treaty, a prospector named James Marshall discovered gold near Sutter's Mill (now Sacramento), and the Gold Rush was on.

Although a few priceless nuggets were found, the true wealth of the Gold Rush had less to do with the precious metal than with the speedy settlement of the brand-new American territory and the development of the "California mythology."

A motley crew of Americans, Asians, Mexicans, English, and French—the Forty-Niners, as they were called—came in droves to the region, and the population grew sixfold within four years. The miners' demands for food, entertainment, and supplies created an economic boom in the region, sparking San Francisco's development as an international port, Sacramento's growth to the point where it ultimately became California's capital city, and California's almost instantaneous statehood in 1850. But many frontier and mining towns bloomed like vivid annual flowers, then died within a generation. (Bodie, for example, boasted ten thousand inhabitants, sixty-five saloons, and one murder per day in its heyday in the 1880s. Today it is a true ghost town.)

In the latter part of the nineteenth century, although the deluge tapered off, eastern settlers con-

**THIS BOY, IN HIS NATIVE COSTUME**
*(above), and these Sumo wrestlers (left), displaying
their strength, are enjoying the pleasures of the annual
Japanese Cherry Blossom Festival in San Francisco.*

tinued to pour into the state. The completion of the transcontinental railroad in 1868 encouraged even more settlers to head west. One sad result of the rapid settlement was the decimation of the Native Americans, who had populated the region for centuries. Unlike the Spanish padres, or even the rancheros, the new settlers instigated Indian wars and brought disease and famine. Between 1850 and 1875, California's Native American population was reduced by more than seventy-five percent.

California continued to grow radically throughout the twentieth century. (In 1900, the population of the state was about 1,500,000; today it is close to thirty million.) Southern Calfornia, particularly the area around Los Angeles, enjoyed the greatest development. The year-round warm climate, the golden sun, the exquisite foliage, and the cheap real estate for many years lured businesses (especially the movie business) and middle-class Americans searching for a new "Promised Land." The advent of the automobile surely helped. (Dividing lines on highways and automatic traffic signals started in L.A.)

But other areas also prospered. Once a constructive form of irrigation was conceived, California's Central Valley boomed, turning California into the leading agriculture state in the nation, with oranges, grapes, dates,

61

SURFING IS CALIFORNIA'S
*signature sport—thanks, in
large part, to the popularity of
the 1960s melodies of the ever-
popular Beach Boys.*

*BESIDES EXCELLENT SKIING, SNOW hiking is a favored winter activity in the Sierras, the Cascades, and the southern Sierras near Los Angeles.*

avocados, artichokes, tomatoes, cotton, and grains being the primary crops. During World War II, the machinery and airplane industries, and other transportation equipment businesses, flourished, continuing to thrive even after the war was over. Fields of petroleum and natural gas today yield thousands of barrels of fuel a day and make California a leading mining state.

It was not until the late 1960s, after California emerged as America's most populous state, that a few cracks began to show as a result of such rapid development. California college students, notably those at the University of California at Berkeley, revolted. Ghettos, such as Watts, in Los Angeles, exploded. Migrant workers went on strike as a result of poor working conditions. In the 1970s, California was besieged with water and fuel shortages, smog, and tax crunches. In the 1980s, previously unknown diseases such as AIDS decimated entire segments of the population. Businesses that had prospered a few short years before—such as the computer business that had created Silicon Valley—began to soften. California completed the 1980s with one of the biggest earthquakes in its history, in October 1989.

But as California enters the last decade of the twentieth century, it seems to be settling into a reluctant, but attractive, middle age. New Age religions, begun in the 1960s with the flower children, still find followers, but with a newfound sense of realism. Environmental protection, a popular issue since the days of John Muir, remains imperative. California has come to terms with its superlatives, accepted its faults, and is ready to face the new millenium.

**FIELDS OF LUSH WILDFLOWERS CAN BE FOUND THROUGHOUT**
*California from the Redwood country in the north, to the Central Valley,*
*to the arid south.*

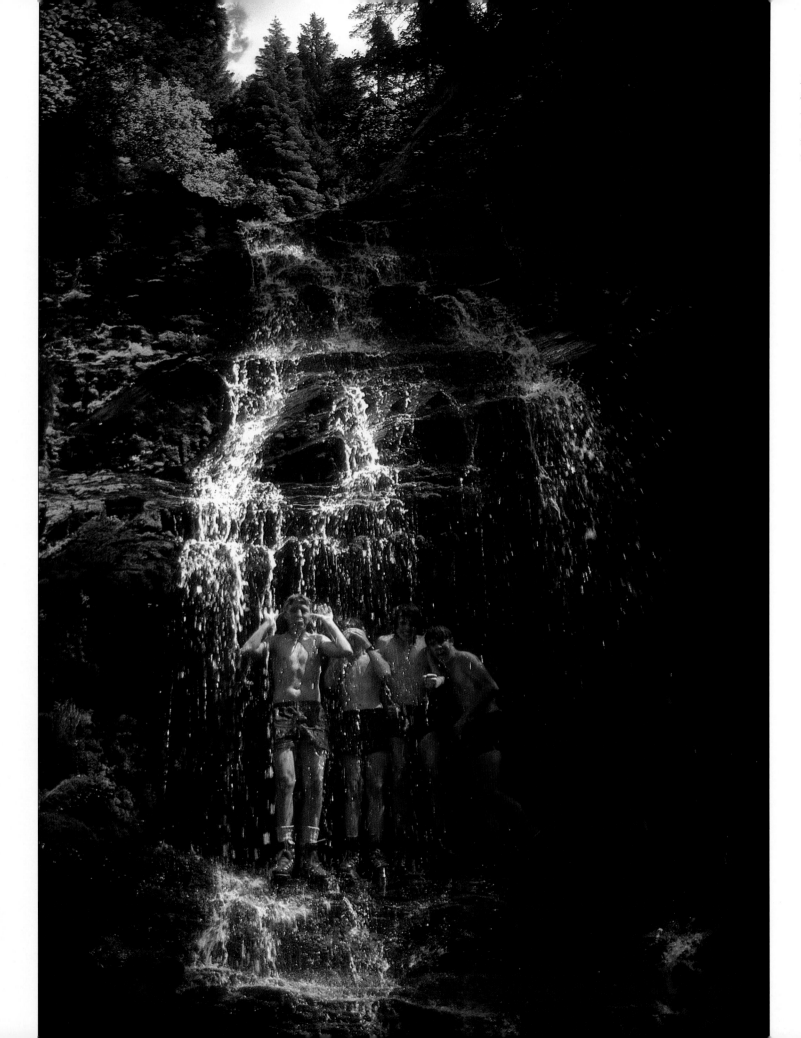

EXQUISITE WATERFALLS
*such as this one on Marble
Mountain in Northern
California add majesty and
mystery to many California
mountain regions.*

65

## The "Golden" State

Prior to Spanish colonization in the eighteenth century, most of California's population consisted of various small tribes of Native Americans. The Spanish friars arrived with the notion of converting the Indians to Christianity and helping them to establish a more "civilized" existence. After Mexican independence, the conquistadors set up the vast ranches, and although the population remained sparse, most of the inhabitants were of Spanish or Mexican decent.

It was in the 1840s that European and American colonists began to arrive, first in a trickle to farm the fertile land in the north or to mill in the vast forests, and a few years later, in a deluge to search for gold. Along with these adventurers came thousands of Chinese, Japanese, and Mexican workers in search of jobs.

Those—primarily white—men who made a fortune either in gold, or more likely, in related and shrewd business dealings, became the California aristocrats, and they established mansions on Nob Hill or estates in the rural valleys. Although the Chinese and Japanese laborers realized their services were no longer needed after the Gold Rush boom, they managed to establish their own enclaves and created an independent culture. The Mexican workers were not so lucky and to this day suffer from labor discrimination.

But myths are at least partly based in reality, and the California golden girl image developed from that myth-making machine, Hollywood. After the birth of the motion picture, glowing beautiful faces of every age were projected on screens across America, and many of these became synonymous with California life. Such stars as Mary Pickford, Shirley Temple, Doris Day, and Marilyn Monroe encouraged the myth.

Even the male actors of Hollywood's golden years—Charlie Chaplin, Douglas Fairbanks, Cary Grant, Humphrey Bogart, and Rock Hudson—most of whom had not grown up in California, still contributed to the Hollywood image. Indeed, the stereotype became so entrenched in the American psyche that a California actor was elected to the presidency of the United States. (It is interesting to note that the terms of office of two presidents from California, Richard

THIS YOUNG WOMAN IN
*her hip garb, standing before
an avant-garde mural in Los
Angeles, serves as a perfect
symbol of contemporary
Southern California life.*

NEON SIGNS ARE ONE
*of the more popular forms
of art and advertising in
California. This one (previous
page), illuminating a
restaurant in Long Beach,
succeeds in appearing both
elegant and funky.*

69

*THIS SWIMMING POOL at San Simeon hints at the opulence of William Randolph Hearst's La Casa Grande, the main house.*

Nixon and Ronald Reagan, have covered sixteen of the last twenty-two years of American political history.)

Californians are proud of their contributions to American life, and these gifts go far beyond the offerings of the silver screen. California writers, painters, photographers, and architects have all made valuable contributions to American culture. F. Scott Fitzgerald, Bret Harte, Mark Twain, Nathaniel West, and Frank Norris all chronicled aspects of California life, while natives such as John Steinbeck, Raymond Chandler, Joan Didion, Dashiell Hammett, Robinson Jeffers, Kenneth Rexroth, and Maxine Hong Kingston have each created California literary classics of sorts. In the late nineteenth century, John Muir wrote exquisite essays about the California landscape. Even today, new

writers such as Sue Grafton are detailing the Southern California lifestyle—with many of its flaws—as the state forges on into the 1990s.

West Coast artists have played an important role in the history of American art. Such painters as Clyfford Still in his abstract canvases, or minimalist Robert Irwin, and sculptors such as Mark de Suvero or Richard Serra have captured the California personality in fresh ways. Photographers have been equally important, from Dorothea Lange portraying the working and living conditions of migrant workers in the 1930s, to Ansel Adams's astonishing visions of Yosemite.

In the last ten years, nowhere has California shown its deepest creativity more than in the food and wine industry. California has become the center of innova-

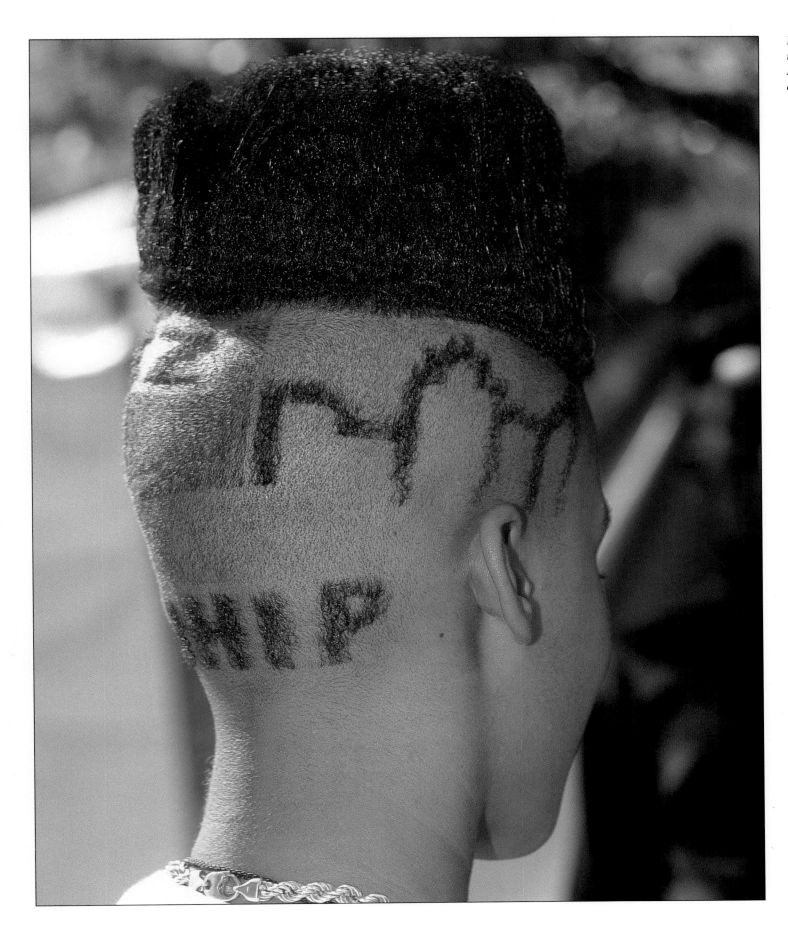

**LOS ANGELES HAS BEEN**
*the birthplace of many*
*American trends—including*
*exotic hairstyles.*

MANHATTAN BEACH AND *Hermosa Beach, south of L.A., are the "home" of beach volleyball. The Manhattan Beach Open is the Wimbledon of the sport.*

**GRAUMAN'S CHINESE**
*Theatre (now Mann's Chinese Theatre) in Los Angeles serves as Hollywood's answer to an ancient Chinese temple. (It is, in fact, a movie house.) The pavement in front of its doors has recorded the hand, foot, paw, and even nose (Jimmy Durante's) prints of "Hollywood Stars" since 1927.*

tive American cuisine. Many Americans, particularly jaded easterners, joke about California's natural food fads, including such oddities as blue corn tortillas and ersatz Mexican fare. But California cooking, exemplified by such artisans as Alice Waters of Chez Panisse, Bradley Ogden of Postrio, Wolfgang Puck of Spago, and a few select others, represents the creative combination of California's agricultural bounty.

The wine industry has also flourished. California grapes and wines such as Cabernet Sauvignon, Merlot, Pinot Noir, Chardonnay, and Sauvignon Blanc have become not only accepted, but sometimes preferred over European varieties thoughout the world. Vintners, from the venerated Robert Mondavi to the maverick fellows at Stag's Leap, have taken the "gold" from California's grapes and used it with imagination.

## The California Life-style

Californians are perhaps best known for their "life-style." Sailboats, fast cars, surfboards, skateboards, tennis courts, swimming pools, beachfront homes, and hot-air balloons are just a few of the trappings of the California "life-style." In addition, California provides the most beautiful scenery in the world to play in.

For campers, hikers, or river rafters, there is the entire stretch of the Sierras, not to mention the Cascades. Skiers, whether downhill or cross country, can find snowy expanses for schussing and gliding. Rock climbers and spelunkers (those who like to explore caves) have ample rocky terrain to tackle.

Golfers challenge the most spectacular courses in the world at Pebble Beach on the Monterey Peninsula,

*THE HAND AND FOOT prints of Marilyn Monroe, herself a personification of the "California Dream" and the "Hollywood Star."*

**SKATEBOARDING IS YET**
*another popular sport,
particularly in Southern
California and especially
among the younger,
more limber, set.*

CALIFORNIA IS HOME TO *a myriad of nationalities and cultures. This Asian-American boy mirrors the beauty of this rainbow civilization.*

*A SURFER WITH HIS*
*board enjoys the golden*
*sun before catching an*
*awesome wave.*

as well as further south near Palm Springs. For those who prefer simply to watch sports, California again has emerged supreme in the area of spectator sports, with a powerhouse baseball team (the Oakland Athletics), a famous basketball team (the Los Angeles Lakers), a great ice hockey team, a world-class volleyball team, and, of course, the grandfather of them all, the Rose Bowl Football game.

Yet of all the recreational choices available in California, the beach reigns supreme. For swimming, snorkeling, surfing, windsurfing, sailing, running, jogging, even volleyball or Frisbee, California has literally hundreds of astonishingly beautiful sandy shores. The beach is so intrinsic to the California life-style that in some places, an entire beach culture has developed.

Recreation is born of the word "re-create." For most of its people, California is about re-creating. From the beginning, explorers, Spanish friars, Forty-Niners, and movie stars all trekked to the golden land of opportunity, California, to re-create themselves. Now, at the end of the twentieth century, the most ingenious Californians are taking the land, the cities, the people, and their visions and re-creating them into realities that will no doubt be appreciated by dreamers the world around.

THE TOURNAMENT OF ROSES PARADE, WHICH WINDS THROUGH THE
*streets of Pasadena on New Year's Day, provides the preview for the Rose Bowl football
game. The outstanding floats are covered with thousands of beautiful flowers.*

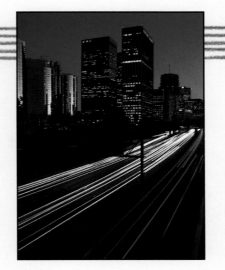

# THE CITIES

The urban centers of California call to mind almost as many superlatives as the physical land. Many of California's towns have developed in rare harmony with nature, and like the California landscape, they are varied, interesting, and in many cases, spectacularly beautiful. This is no less true of California's great urban centers than it is of its small villages.

In fact, California is home to four of the nation's twenty largest cities. In descending order of population, these are: Los Angeles, San Diego, as a curious result of the development of the silicon chip, San Jose, and San Francisco. Like all cities, rhyme and reason lurk behind their development, but like the rich and varied California landscape, the cities are unique unto themselves. San Francisco is as different from Los Angeles as Paris is from Rome; San Jose is in many ways the antithesis of

San Diego. Like Paris and Rome, all the cities of California are equally loved and equally valued, but their personalities could not be more diverse.

## San Francisco

San Francisco is not only California's most charming and beautiful city, it is one of the most enchanting cities in the world. Famed for its hills, cable cars, and breathtaking Golden Gate Bridge—which spans the even more glorious San Francisco Bay—San Francisco sits on a throne of perfection. As any native will attest, San Francisco rests in an ideal place, possesses a perfect climate, and hosts a fascinating and friendly population.

San Francisco was first occupied by the Spanish in 1776. They founded a mission in the name of the King of Spain and dedicated it to Saint Francis. The city became Mexican when that country achieved independence in 1821. The United States occupied the Presidio in 1846 during the Mexican-American War, then the 1849 Gold Rush made San Francisco one of America's busiest ports literally overnight. It was declared the capital of California in 1850.

Over the next fifty years, until the turn of the twentieth century, San Francisco reigned as America's most alluring city, serving as a focal point for Americans who yearned to "go west." At the same time, it developed into an important port as farming and logging became big businesses in California.

During the early years of the twentieth century, Los Angeles began to develop, competing with San Francisco for the role of California's premier city. But during those years, San Francisco matured into the "grande dame" of the West, and today it remains a city of sophisticated charm, compared to L.A.'s brash brilliance.

Over the years, San Francisco has played many roles. During World War II, San Francisco served as the center for all United States Pacific operations; during the 1950s, it played hostess to the "beat generation"; and in the 1960s, its Haight-Ashbury flower children were at the center of the hippie movement. For the last

**THE SKYLINE OF**
*Los Angeles, the "City of Angeles," can at times appear to be a bed of twinkling rhinestones (page 84–85).*

**THE REFLECTION OF**
*automobile lights and the glitter of L.A.'s modern buildings create the look of America in the last decade of the twentieth century (page 85).*

**THE MAJESTIC GOLDEN**
*Gate Bridge emerges from the ubiquitous San Francisco fog.*

**THE TRANSAMERICA**
*Pyramid, the most*
*"earthquake-proof" structure*
*in downtown San Francisco,*
*has added a distinctive look to*
*the city's skyline since 1972.*

CABLE CARS, WHICH WERE DECLARED A HISTORIC LANDMARK
*in 1964, are one of San Francisco's most popular attractions and stand as a symbol of that
city's uniqueness.*

PARKS, INCLUDING
*Golden Gate Park and the
serene area at the top of
Telegraph Hill, are rich with
flora that add to San
Francisco's romance.*

two decades, San Francisco has established itself as the center of cultural sophistication in California, a mecca for lovers of good art, music, dance, and food.

San Francisco lies some four hundred miles (640 km) south of the Oregon border, or about one-third of the way down the state. The city itself lies at the northern tip of a peninsula that separates San Francisco Bay from the Pacific Ocean. The Golden Gate strait, which is spanned by San Francisco's magnificent red bridge, is actually the city's gateway to the sea.

San Francisco is characteristically hilly and is surrounded by water on three sides. Most of the city's attractions are located near the wharf area at the northeast edge of the peninsula, in a triangle formed by Van Ness Avenue, Market Street, and the Embarcadero, or waterfront. Like New York City, San Francisco is often described in terms of its neighborhoods, which include North Beach, the Mission District, Chinatown, Nob Hill, Pacific Heights, and the Financial District.

At the top of the wedge is North Beach, a district inhabited predominantly by Italian-Americans, artists, and "yuppies." The focal point of North Beach is Telegraph Hill, topped by Coit Tower, one of San Francisco's identifying landmarks. Known also as the "Latin Quarter" and "Little Italy," North Beach was home to the bohemian "beats" in the 1950s, and the City Lights Bookstore still draws interested poets and writers.

Down the Embarcadero from North Beach is Fisherman's Wharf, now one of the city's famous tourist attractions. Ghirardelli Square, home of the chocolate factory, The Cannery—a mini-mall transformed from a fish-processing plant, and a cluster of trendy restaurants make this area the Quincy Market of San Francisco. The notorious prison, Alcatraz, looms on its namesake island in the distance.

In the early days of San Francisco's development, the neighborhoods of Nob Hill and Russian Hill were home to the shrewd entrepreneurs who made their fortunes as a result of the Gold Rush. The streets were lined with ornate Victorian mansions, and happily, many remain. Nob Hill and Russian Hill today are home to "old San Franciscans"—and probably to a few new ones as well. Elegant Grace Cathedral sits at the top of the hill.

**VICTORIAN HOUSES LINE THE**
*hilly streets of many of San Francisco's
neighborhoods, especially Pacific Heights
and the Mission District.*

92

**MANY OF SAN FRANCISCO'S ELEGANT VICTORIAN HOMES**
*have received a coat of California's distinct color and artistry.*

94

THE STREETS OF
San Francisco's Chinatown are
lined with authentic Chinese
restaurants that serve
traditional—and delectable—
Oriental fare.

MANY DELIGHTFUL INNS,
such as the Magnolia Hotel
(right), pictured here, dot
Napa Valley, welcoming
visitors to America's finest
wine-growing region.

One of the most fascinating streets zigzagging down this wave of hills is the famous Lombard Street, located between Hyde and Leavenworth streets. Lombard Street was "created" in the 1920s in order to allow carriages to negotiate the remarkably steep hill. Each curve is now planted with colorful flowers. Even today, in a car with good brakes, the ride is breathtaking.

San Francisco's Chinatown, probably one of America's first Oriental enclaves, covers an area of about twenty-four square blocks and is today the most densely populated of San Francisco's neighborhoods. Founded in the 1880s, Chinatown was established by Chinese immigrants who had labored in the gold mines and had laid railroad track west. Victims of racism, they found it necessary to band together for protection. The Chinatown Gate spans Grant Avenue at the southern entrance to the neighborhood, announcing with pride the Chinese stronghold.

The Financial District lies east of Chinatown and south of North Beach, with Montgomery Street functioning as the "Wall Street of the West." San Francisco's most distinct structure, the 853-foot (260-m) Trans-America Pyramid, stands at Montgomery Street between Clay and Washington. Designed by the architectural firm William Pereira and Associates on a lark, the building's pyramidal shape makes it one of the city's most earthquake-resistant buildings. Across from the pyramid is the Old TransAmerica Building, and a few blocks away is the Pacific Stock Exchange. The Embarcadero Center, spanning three full blocks, features an abundance of shops, restaurants, and urban park areas. Office buildings tower above. Business people scurry to work, stopping only purchase a European-style capuccino from one of the many coffee carts along the way.

Union Square is considered the center of the downtown area, with the regal St. Francis Hotel holding forth on one side of the square. Discriminating shoppers will find all the merchandise they seek here.

The Mission District, Pacific Heights, and the Marina are attractive residential areas replete with beautifully restored houses and trendy restaurants. The Marina came into the spotlight in October 1989,

95

when a strong earthquake shook the Marina district much more dramatically than any other neighborhood in San Francisco. Though this neighborhood's buildings are built for the most part, on landfill, its bloodlines held, and within months, even this hard-hit area was back on its feet.

## Bay Area Towns

Surrounding San Francisco—with a quick crossing of either the Golden Gate Bridge or the Bay Bridge—rest various towns, each with a history and personality all its own.

Sausalito, just across the Golden Gate, is a hill town and possesses all the allure of an Italian seacoast village. It sits on Richardson Bay at the southern end of Marin County. The town's waterfront street is lined with shops and restaurants, and its harbor is full of small vessels of various sizes and shapes. Its hillside homes are beautiful, and many boast a spectacular view of San Francisco Bay.

Sausalito has always been closely connected to San Francisco. A ferry runs between the two cities, and it continues as an efficient form of communication for those living in Marin County, and a favorite tourist attraction for visitors to San Francisco. Although Sausalito is tied to the larger city, it retains a unique style.

Opposite Richardson Bay from Sausalito sits Tiburon. Like Sausalito, Tiburon has managed to maintain its separate identity, witnessed by its one-hundred-year-old Main Street, which remains just as it originally was. Tiburon, to many, symbolizes the California good life.

Just minutes north of San Francisco lie the Marin Headlands, now part of the Golden Gate National Recreation Area, with remarkably beautiful valleys and windswept beaches—a gateway to California's Northern Coast splendor.

Oakland is the East Bay's major city. The third largest city in Northern California, Oakland is an important industrial center and shipping port. It also prides itself on its recreation areas, impressive sports complex, and of course, its impressive baseball team,

*AN AWE-INSPIRING VIEW of San Francisco Bay from atop the cabled Golden Gate Bridge.*

**SAUSALITO'S YACHT CLUB,** *the focal point of this quaint and scenic town, sits near the Golden Gate, across the bay from regal San Francisco.*

OCEAN BEACH PIER IN SAN DIEGO AT SUNSET.

the Oakland Athletics.

Berkeley also lies to the east of San Francisco and is home to one of the world's largest and most prestigious educational institutions, the University of California at Berkeley, known popularly simply as "Berkeley." Known for its fine restaurants, particularly Chez Panisse; its distinctive Maybeck-inspired architecture; its interesting repertory theater; and its Shoreline Park and Marina, Berkeley adds an intellectual dimension to the Bay Area in which its residents take pride.

## San Jose

San Jose, California's third largest city, lies at the southern end of San Francisco Bay and is the center of the renowned Silicon Valley, the birthplace of the computer chip. It's a clean, efficient, attractive place with mild, clear, sunny weather—an ideal place to live.

San Jose claims a two-hundred-year-old history, one of the twenty-one missions established by the Spanish.

Mission Santa Clara de Asis is a fine replica. Winchester Mystery House, the home of Sarah Winchester, heir to the Winchester gun fortune, lures tourists to the abode that Mrs. Winchester believed was haunted by all the men ever killed by the Winchester rifle.

Two important college towns, Santa Cruz and Palo Alto are located near San Jose. Palo Alto is home to Stanford University. The university's somewhat bookish atmosphere, replete with fine faculty, bright students, avant-garde galleries, and arty film houses, is offset by beautiful homes, luxurious cars, and chic shops. The town also benefits from the prosperity of Hewlett-Packard and other important technical firms.

Santa Cruz is considered by some to be the "hippest" town on the California coast, the direct result of its seaside location and the University of California at Santa Cruz. Although the university is not quite as revered as Stanford or Berkeley, it is a fine institution of liberal learning, and the town's beach and boardwalk offer a "beach life" that is one of the best on the coast.

## Los Angeles

If San Francisco is the "grand dame" of the Pacific Coast, then L.A. is the rebellious adolescent—glitzy, hip, trendy, and ready-to-roll. For many people, Los Angeles is the "star" of California. Indeed, not only is it California's largest city, but it is the second largest city in the United States—the West Coast's answer to New York. When one thinks of California, one's mind jumps to the clichéd images of L.A.—sunshine, smog, palm trees, buzzing freeways, lavish homes, swimming pools, beach bums, starlets, and movie moguls.

Actually Los Angeles is not a centralized city at all, but a cluster of urban substructures connected by L.A.'s web of freeways and almost notorious thoroughfares, such as Sunset Boulevard, Wilshire Boulevard, and of course, Hollywood Boulevard. Whether it is Hollywood, Beverly Hills, Pasadena, Malibu, Venice, Bel-Air, or Sherman Oaks, each suburb has its own identity.

Los Angeles was founded in 1781 by eleven Spanish families sent from Mexico to develop the land along the Los Angeles River. The village was named El Pueblo de Nuestra Señora la Reina de Los Angeles, or The Town of Our Lady the Queen of the Angels. Although Los Angeles is considered to be a Pacific Coast city because many of its most celebrated suburbs —such as Santa Monica and Venice—are beach towns, initially the village was located many miles inland. It wasn't until after World War I, when the automobile began to erase distances, that villages such as Malibu—or even Beverly Hills—were considered anything more than places to which Los Angeles natives trekked for a day in the sun.

Vestiges of the original village, or "pueblo," have been preserved around Olvera Street, near "downtown" Los Angeles. The Plaza was once the center of the town and remains the heart of the refurbished pueblo. Olvera Street, a block-long brick pedestrian lane, provides a hint of the original market. Other structures such as the Old Plaza Fire House, the Union Passenger Terminal, the Civic Center, and the Plaza Church tell the history of Los Angeles—not simply her Mexican and Spanish heritage, but her twentieth-century revival.

103

LOS ANGELES IS NOT SO
*much a unified city as it is a
collection of unique suburbs
connected by a web of
freeways.*

OLVERA STREET (RIGHT), one of the last remaining streets from the original pueblo of Los Angeles, is the site of Cinco de Mayo, the festival marking Mexican independence. The red, white, and green banner with the "bear" insignia is California's state flag.

UNION STATION (FAR right), built in the 1930s, is one of the last great railway stations erected in the United States. Its adobe facade, tower, and arches exemplify the romance of old Los Angeles.

**LIKE THE STATUE OF** *Liberty or Big Ben, the rather tattered Hollywood sign that stands fifty feet (15 m) high on a mountainside north of Hollywood, is a symbol of the faded glamour of that town.*

In fact, downtown Los Angeles has enjoyed something of a renaissance in recent years. As of 1957, tall structures could legally be built, and thus a few towering office buildings, and several museums, parks, and shopping areas give the city a small sense of centeredness. However, Los Angeles will always be perceived as the quintessential example of "urban sprawl."

Since it came to maturity in the 1920s and 1930s, Los Angeles has been most famous for its "suburban" pockets, with Hollywood, Beverly Hills, Pasadena, and the various beach towns having the most distinctive personalities.

Hollywood Boulevard is the best known of all L.A.'s thoroughfares for the simple reason that it leads directly to Hollywood, the mythical home of the "stars." The large "Hollywood" sign, which was erected to encourage a real-estate venture, tells visitors in no uncertain terms that they have arrived. The sidewalk along Hollywood Boulevard itself is studded with bronze stars and the names of film, radio, and television actors and actresses who have given Hollywood its special flavor. Grauman's (now Mann's) Chinese Theatre, a classic Hollywood venture opened in 1927, is best known not as a cinema, but for the autographs of the movie stars engraved in the cement in front.

Sadly, despite all of Hollywood's fame, it is now a rather seedy place. Its own "day in the sun" has passed, and the moguls now make their deals in plush offices in Century City or other removed and hermetically sealed places. Nevertheless, the glamorous ghosts of Hollywood's past seem to lurk in the shadows.

Like Hollywood, Beverly Hills, which lies west of downtown Los Angeles, had its first heyday in the 1920s and 1930s, when newly rich movie folk built audacious homes along the town's curvy, quiet streets. (Unlike Hollywood, Beverly Hills remains L.A.'s chicest suburb.) The Beverly Hills Hotel, the glamorous pink elephant that sits in great splendor on Sunset Boulevard, has played a large role in creating the Beverly Hills mystique. Under the direction of Hernando Courtright— one of the world's greatest hoteliers—actors, moguls, politicians, and socialites were lured to the luxury of the hotel—and later its glittering Polo Lounge—and, as a result, to Beverly Hills, itself.

*THE GLAMOROUS BUNKER Hill Offices in "downtown" Los Angeles are one example of the city's late twentieth-century urban rejuvenation.*

The suburban sprawl that makes up Los Angeles seems to be growing endlessly. Beautiful Southern California beach towns such as Malibu, Santa Monica, Venice, Marina Del Ray, Redondo Beach, Hermosa Beach, and Palos Verdes are all desirable places to live, but like Los Angeles itself, they suffer from the growing pains common to developing urban areas. In recent years, Santa Monica has even played host to a rather vociferous homeless population.

As Los Angeles continues to grow, its tentacles spread down the coast, reaching even into surrounding counties. Long Beach, once considered far away, is now but a short jaunt on the freeway from L.A. Disneyland, the granddaddy of theme parks, was built in the 1950s "far out" in Orange County. But today, when one thinks of L.A., one naturally includes Disneyland—and nearby Knotts Berry Farm—as part of the vista.

Los Angeles is the city—the "place"—that best symbolizes American life in the mid-twentieth century. In 1910, the movie business and the automobile industry were both in their infancy, but both came to maturity in Los Angeles and to a great degree, influenced and shaped the city. Much that is attractive about the West Coast—gorgeous weather, beautiful homes, an easygoing life-style—can be found in L.A. At the same time, however, much that is troubling—crime, drugs, environmental destruction, and a certain weariness of spirit—can also be found there. In many ways, Los Angeles has not quite come of age, but the manner in which its problems are eventually solved will indicate its maturity.

Rodeo Drive is today the Fifth Avenue of Beverly Hills, lined with the world's most glorious shops, including Gucci, Bijan, and Giorgio's. At the top of Rodeo Drive sits the regal Beverly Wilshire Hotel, another Hernando Courtright creation, which gives the entire area a sense of quality and luxury.

Despite its wealth and glamour, Beverly Hills is sometimes perceived as slightly vulgar. It is the town of Pasadena that represents the old money and quality of Los Angeles. A wealthy and attractive suburb with decidedly Spanish overtones, Pasadena is home not only to L.A.'s more established folk, but also to California's most famous annual event, the Rose Bowl.

AN AERIAL VIEW OF THE
Rose Bowl in Pasadena.
The Rose Bowl football
tournament is one of
California's oldest and most
venerated sporting events.

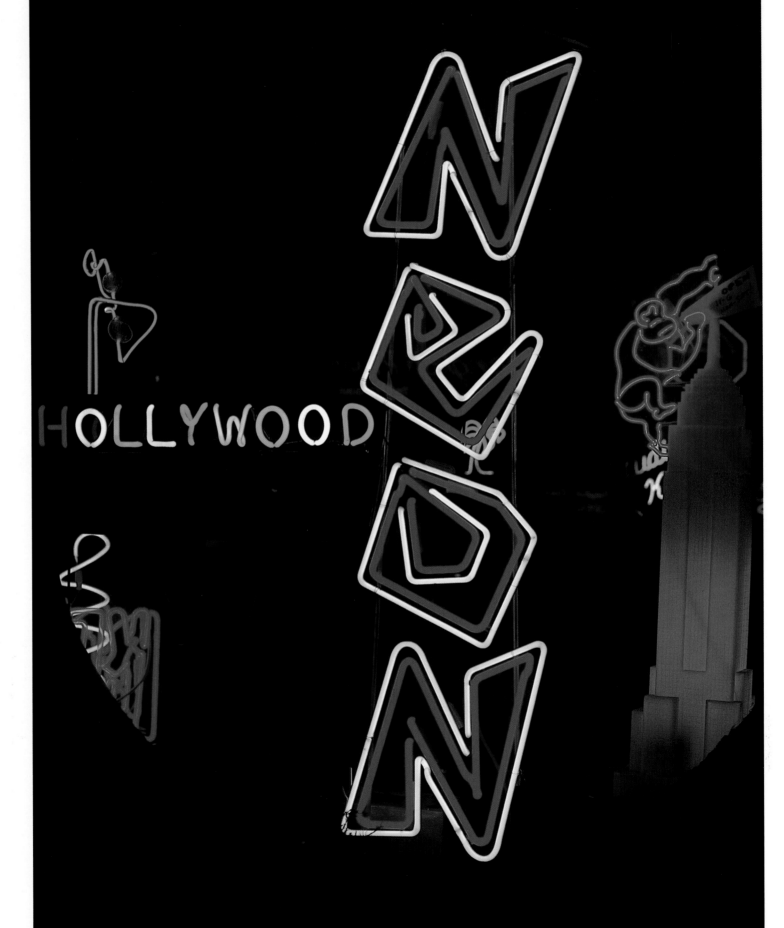

**NEON SIGNS HAVE** *become extremely popular for advertising, particularly in California.*

CITY HALL

the
BURGER
THAT ATE
LA

113

LOS ANGELES IS KNOWN
*for its innovative —*
*and sometimes funky —*
*architecture. These fast food*
*joints are a few examples of*
*the inspiration sunshine*
*brings.*

**CRANES LOADING SHIPS AT THE** *port of Los Angeles at dusk remind natives and visitors alike that Los Angeles is more than just a haven for beach bums and movie moguls.*

**VENICE, THE FIRST TOWN SOUTH OF SANTA MONICA, IS HOME TO THE**
*most unique beach culture in Southern California. Once the town was striated with*
*glamorous canals, but today Venice is enjoying a rejuvenation of a different sort.*

The Rose Bowl is the scene of the football game between the winners of the Big Ten and the Pacific Ten college football teams. The Tournament of Roses Parade, its colorful floats decorated with banks of flowers, is held in Pasadena on New Year's Day, before the game.

## San Diego

Not only is San Diego California's second largest city in population, but like Los Angeles, it holds an important position on the Southern California coastline. However, despite its balmy climate and Southern California atmosphere, San Diego is nothing like Los Angeles.

Located about ninety miles (145 km) south of Los Angeles and the same distance north of the Mexican border, San Diego has been referred to as "America's Finest City"—an appellation that would never be applied to Los Angeles. It claims clean air, perfect weather (except for a few days in June), and a general sense of prosperity evidenced by its beautiful homes.

Like other attractive towns on the California coast, San Diego was first established by the Yuman Indians and later settled by the Spanish, in 1769. San Diego was basically bypassed by the booms that built San Francisco in the nineteenth century and Los Angeles in the early twentieth, but with two international expositions (one in 1915, and one in 1935) and the establishment of a U.S. Navy presence during and after World War II, San Diego grew.

Today it boasts a number of fascinating tourist attractions, especially Balboa Park with its fabulous zoo, Old Town San Diego with its reconstructed Spanish settlement, the Gas Light District and its beautifully restored Victorian homes, and the well-known Sea World. Naturally, San Diego is not without beaches, which are as beautiful as those found further up the coast. Its suburbs, especially La Jolla, one of the most attractive towns in the entire state, are very special.

Because it is the center of the defense industry and boasts one of the largest navy yards, San Diego has grown in population and importance. It is one of California's conventional cities—conservative and refined—and comfortable with that reputation.

**FIELDS OF POPPIES**
*grow profusely in open sunny fields, and, as the California state flower, pay tribute to the golden sun, golden tans, and, of course, the gold that brought many Americans to the West.*

THE TOWER AT THE
University of California, San
Diego, creates the focal point
for one of the most gracious
college campuses in the state.

SAN DIEGO, KNOWN AS "AMERICA'S FINEST CITY," IS CURRENTLY THE
*proud home of the America's Cup trophy, the highest sailing honor, at the*
*San Diego Yacht Club.*

SUNRISE OVER THE
Sierra Crest, which runs along
the eastern border of Sequoia
National Park and boasts the
most stunning range of
mountains in the Sierra
Nevadas.

123

# INDEX

125